CAREER SUCCESS TIDBITS®: MODERN EDITION

CAREER RESILIENCE & WELLNESS

Ella L. Clark

Staying Grounded, Effective, and Well in a Changed World of Work

By

Ella L. Clark

The Clark Group, LLC

Copyright © 2026 Ella L. Clark,

All rights reserved.

No part of this publication may be reproduced, stored in a retrieval system, or transmitted in any form or by any means, electronic, mechanical, photocopy, recording, or otherwise, without the prior written permission of the author, except for brief quotations used in reviews or educational materials.

This book is a work of nonfiction. Names, characters, businesses, places, events, and incidents are either the product of the author's imagination or used in a fictitious manner. Any resemblance to actual people, living or dead, or actual events is purely coincidental.

ISBN: 978-8-9947626-2-2

Published by:

The Clark Group, LLC [City, State]

www.clarkgroupcoaching.com

DEDICATION

This book honors young people and adults who have managed to find their way in life and achieve career success, even when the route was uncertain.

To those who have had to advocate for themselves, adapt to changing systems, manage unseen challenges, and persist with courage and dignity, your resilience has been my greatest teacher.

This book is also meant for professionals returning to workplaces that are different than before, facing increased responsibilities, and working hard to remain effective, optimistic, and resilient despite uncertain circumstances.

May these pages affirm your experience, strengthen your voice, and remind you that success does not require the sacrifice of your well-being.

ACKNOWLEDGMENTS

Meaningful work is never accomplished in isolation. I am grateful to the youth and adults who have trusted me with their stories, challenges, and aspirations. Your bravery, determination, and ability to navigate systems that were not always created with you in mind have deepened my understanding of what it truly means to be resilient, to advocate for yourself, and to achieve meaningful success. I extend sincere appreciation to the educators, counselors, administrators, community partners, and fellow coaches who have collaborated with me over the years. Your dedication to fostering growth, inclusion, and opportunity has strengthened this work in ways that cannot be fully captured here.

Thank you to my colleagues, mentors, and leaders who have challenged my thinking, supported my vision, and reminded me that leadership and wellness are inseparable. Your insight and encouragement have helped refine both my voice and my purpose.

Finally, I thank my family and friends for their patience, support, and belief in this journey. Your presence has been a steady source of grounding and perspective.

This book reflects all of you.

Coach Ella Clark

Contents

DEDICATION iii
ACKNOWLEDGMENTS iv
SERIES ORIENTATION vi
HOW TO USE THIS BOOK vii
BOOK SUMMARY viii
PREFACE x
INTRODUCTION xi
CHAPTER ONE 1
When Work Gets Personal 1
CHAPTER TWO 3
Emotional Load vs. Job Description 3
CHAPTER THREE 8
Regulation, Not Suppression 8
CHAPTER FOUR 14
Boundaries, Capacity, and Sustainable Performance 14
CHAPTER FIVE 20
Recovery, Rest, and Rebuilding Energy 20
CHAPTER SIX 25
Communication That Preserves Trust Under Pressure 25
CHAPTER SEVEN 31
Navigating Change Without Losing Yourself 31
CHAPTER EIGHT 36
Confidence, Self-Trust, and Moving Forward 36
CHAPTER NINE 41
Purpose, Meaning, and Staying Engaged 41
CHAPTER TEN 46
Sustaining Yourself Over Time 46
Final Reflection Workbook 50
ABOUT THE AUTHOR 55

SERIES ORIENTATION

How This Book Fits Within the Career Success Tidbits®: Modern Edition Series

The Career Success Tidbits®: Modern Edition series was created to support individuals navigating today's world of work with clarity, confidence, and intention.

Rather than offering one-size-fits-all advice or rigid career formulas, the series recognizes that careers unfold in stages and that different seasons require different kinds of guidance. Each book focuses on a specific aspect of career development, allowing readers to begin where they are and return as their needs evolve.

Together, the three books form a practical progression:

- Book 1: Essential Skills focuses on foundational skills that shape how you show up, including self-awareness, communication, professionalism, and early leadership.

- Book 2: Your Map to Career Freedom centers on navigation, thoughtful decision-making, preparation for change, and moving forward with intention when options feel limited or unclear.

- Book 3: Career Resilience & Wellness addresses sustainability, emphasizing confidence, adaptability, and balance over time, particularly during periods of disruption or transition.

Each book stands on its own and may be read independently. At the same time, the series is designed to work together, offering guidance that grows with you as your career and life circumstances change.

This approach reflects a simple truth: career growth is not linear, and no single book can address every season.

The Career Success Tidbits®: Modern Edition series is intended to serve as a companion, supporting you wherever you are, without pressure to rush or conform to a single path.

This book focuses on sustaining confidence, adaptability, and well-being over the long term, particularly during periods of uncertainty or change.

HOW TO USE THIS BOOK

This book is designed to be both practical and reflective. It is not meant to be rushed or read as a checklist. Instead, it offers guidance you can return to as your work, life, and circumstances evolve.

Each chapter focuses on a core aspect of Career Resilience & Wellness, including managing emotional load, navigating change, setting boundaries, communicating effectively, and sustaining well-being over time. While the chapters build upon one another, you may read them sequentially or begin with the topics most relevant to your current situation.

As you move through the book, you will encounter:

- Realistic workplace insights grounded in today's post-COVID environment.

- Practical strategies you can apply immediately.

- Reflection prompts designed to help you connect concepts to your own experiences.

- Coach Ella Says insights that offer perspective drawn from years of coaching and leadership work.

You are encouraged to pause, reflect, and take notes. Career resilience and wellness are not achieved through perfection or speed, but through awareness, intention, and consistent practice.

This book is for anyone navigating a changed world of work, whether you are early in your career, returning after disruption, supporting others, or redefining success in a new season. Use it as a guide, a reference, and a reminder that effectiveness and well-being can, and should, exist together.

BOOK SUMMARY

Your Map to Career Freedom

Your Map to Career Freedom serves as a steady guide for individuals navigating career decisions during periods of uncertainty, constraint, and change. Rather than promoting dramatic pivots or one-size-fits-all solutions, this book centers on thoughtful movement, helping readers understand where they are, recognize what is influencing their choices, and move forward with intention.

Book Two reframes career freedom as clarity and agency, not escape. It emphasizes that progress often happens gradually, shaped by timing, responsibilities, and real-world conditions. Through practical guidance and reflection, readers are encouraged to pause before acting, distinguish pressure from readiness, and make decisions rooted in awareness rather than urgency.

The book walks readers through key stages of navigation: orienting themselves within their current reality, reading signals without rushing to conclusions, expanding options without forcing decisions, and positioning themselves for future opportunity.

It highlights the importance of preparation, perspective, and self-trust, especially when options feel limited or the path ahead is unclear.

Throughout *Your Map to Career Freedom*, readers learn how to evaluate opportunities thoughtfully, engage in meaningful conversations with confidence, and make grounded decisions they can stand behind, even without guarantees.

The focus remains on sustainable forward movement, not perfection or speed. By the conclusion of Book Two, readers are better equipped to understand their position, trust their judgment, and move forward with greater clarity and confidence.

This foundation sets the stage for the next phase of the journey, where sustaining momentum, adaptability, and well-being over time become essential.

PREFACE

Sustaining Confidence and Well-Being Over Time

Careers are not built in straight lines. They unfold through growth, change, uncertainty, and transition. Along the way, many people discover that staying steady is just as important as moving forward.

This book was written for those moments.

You may be navigating ongoing change, recovering from disruption, or simply trying to maintain balance in a demanding environment. You may be successful on paper, yet feeling stretched, tired, or unsure how to sustain momentum without burning out.

Career resilience is not about pushing harder. It is about learning how to manage energy, respond to change, and remain connected to yourself as circumstances shift.

This book offers guidance for sustaining confidence, adaptability, and well-being, so your career can support your life rather than compete with it.

INTRODUCTION

Redefining Resilience in Modern Careers

Resilience is often misunderstood as toughness or endurance. Career resilience centers on awareness, flexibility, and self-management. It involves recognizing when to lean in, when to adjust, and when to protect your energy so you can continue forward with clarity.

In today's work environments, change is constant. Roles evolve, expectations shift, and stability can feel temporary. Without intentional practice, it becomes easy to lose confidence or disconnect from what matters most.

This book invites you to take a steadier approach.

Rather than reacting to every change, you will explore ways to stay grounded, adapt thoughtfully, and build habits that support long-term growth. The focus is not on avoiding stress, but on responding to it with perspective and care.

You do not need to have everything figured out. You need tools that help you remain balanced as you grow.

This book is here to support that journey.

CHAPTER ONE

When Work Gets Personal

There was a time when work and personal life were expected to remain separate.

Employees were encouraged to leave emotions at the door, focus on performance, and push through discomfort. Today, that expectation no longer reflects reality.

Work has become personal.

Health concerns, caregiving responsibilities, financial pressure, identity shifts, and constant change now travel with people into the workplace. These realities do not pause at the office door. They influence focus, energy, communication, and decision-making, often in ways that are invisible to others.

Career resilience begins with acknowledging this truth. The New Nature of Workplace Stress

Workplace stress today extends far beyond workload. It includes emotional load, the ongoing effort required to adapt, regulate emotions, manage relationships, and perform under uncertain conditions. Many professionals are navigating hybrid environments, unreliable technology, and inconsistent systems while being expected to maintain the same level of productivity and engagement.

In some cases, employees are returning to physical workplaces that are not fully prepared for full operations. Facilities that sat vacant for extended periods may lack updated infrastructure, functional technology, or adequate accommodation. Budget constraints often delay improvements, leaving employees to work around limitations quietly and continuously.

When systems are under strain, people carry weight.

This additional load rarely appears in job descriptions or performance reviews, yet it contributes significantly to fatigue, frustration, and disengagement. Over time, individuals may internalize these challenges as personal shortcomings rather than recognizing them as structural realities.

Career resilience and wellness help reframe this experience.

Wellness as a Career Strategy

Wellness is often treated as a personal responsibility or a workplace reward. While self-care and stress management practices are important, they are not sufficient on their own. Career resilience and wellness require a broader approach, one that integrates emotional regulation, boundaries, communication, adaptability, and long-term sustainability.

Career resilience is not about enduring discomfort indefinitely. It is about developing the capacity to respond thoughtfully rather than react emotionally, to adapt without self-erasure, and to sustain performance without burnout.

This book invites a different question:

How can I remain effective and well over time, especially when conditions are imperfect?

That question becomes the foundation for everything that follows.

Coach Ella Says

Resilience is not about pushing harder. It is about leading yourself wisely, especially when the pressure is real.

CHAPTER TWO

Emotional Load vs. Job Description

Most job descriptions outline tasks, responsibilities, and performance expectations.

What they rarely acknowledge is the emotional load that accompanies the work. Emotional load is the ongoing effort required to manage feelings, reactions, relationships, uncertainty, and change while still meeting professional expectations. It includes the mental and emotional energy spent adapting to shifting environments, compensating for system gaps, regulating reactions, and maintaining composure under pressure.

In today's workplace, emotional load has increased significantly, yet it remains invisible.

The Hidden Work People Are Carrying

Post-COVID work environments have introduced new layers of complexity. Many professionals are balancing hybrid schedules, unreliable technology, evolving policies, and inconsistent workplace readiness. Some are returning to physical spaces that are not fully functional due to deferred maintenance or budget limitations. Others are expected to remain productive from home while managing caregiving responsibilities, limited childcare options, and blurred boundaries between work and personal life.

When systems are imperfect, people adapt.

They troubleshoot technology, adjust schedules, absorb disruptions, and fill in gaps quietly to keep work moving forward. Over time, this hidden effort becomes emotionally taxing. Individuals may feel drained, frustrated, or overwhelmed without being able to point to a single cause.

This is not a lack of motivation or professionalism. It is the weight of sustained emotional demand.

Why Emotional Load Matters

Emotional load directly affects how people show up at work. It influences focus, communication, decision-making, energy, and engagement. When emotional load goes unrecognized, individuals often internalize stress as personal failure rather than understanding it as a response to ongoing pressure.

In my work supporting youth and adults navigating additional barriers, including disabilities, I have seen how emotional load accumulates when systems require constant adaptation. Managing energy, advocating for needs, and staying emotionally regulated become daily practice rather than occasional strategies.

These same skills are now essential across today's workforce. Career resilience and wellness begin by naming emotional load, not to dwell on it, but to manage it effectively.

Emotional Load Is Not Weakness

There is a misconception that acknowledging emotional strain signals weakness or lack of resilience. Recognizing emotional load is a sign of self-leadership. It allows individuals to respond intentionally rather than react emotionally.

Ignoring emotional load does not make it disappear. It simply shifts the cost, often toward burnout, disengagement, or declining well-being. Career resilience invites a different approach, awareness without judgment.

Managing Emotional Load in Real Time

Career Resilience & Wellness are built through practical choices made daily, especially when conditions are imperfect.

Pause Before You Personalize

When frustration or fatigue arises, ask yourself: Is this stress coming from the system?

Separating personal performance from structural challenges helps prevent unnecessary self-criticism and restores perspective.

Name the Load

Emotional load grows when it remains vague. Naming it internally or in writing turns stress into usable information.

Examples:

1. "I am managing uncertainty."
2. "I am compensating for limited resources."
3. "I am carrying multiple roles at once."
4. Regulate First, Respond Second
5. Before responding to a challenge:
6. Pause
7. Take a few slow breaths
8. Ground yourself physically
9. Regulation creates space for thoughtful decisions rather than emotional reactions.
10. Adjust Expectations Without Guilt
11. Career resilience includes recognizing when expectations, your own or others', need to be temporarily adjusted. This is not lowering standards. It is aligning effort with capacity.
12. Ask:

13. What is essential right now?

14. What can wait?

15. What support or flexibility is reasonable to request?

16. Protect Recovery Time

17. Emotional load requires recovery. Without it, resilience erodes.

18. Build in:

19. Short breaks

20. Reduced constant availability

21. Routines that allow mental decompression

Recovery is not a reward. It is a requirement.

Coach Ella Says

You do not manage emotional load by pushing harder. You manage it by pausing, prioritizing, and protecting your capacity.

Reflection: Emotional Load Check-In

Take a moment to reflect honestly.

1. What parts of my work require emotional effort beyond my formal responsibilities?

- _____
- _____

2. Where am I compensating for system gaps, uncertainty, or lack of resources?

- _____
- _____

3. How does emotional load show up for me physically, mentally, or emotionally?

   - _____
   - _____

4. What is one boundary, adjustment, or support that could help me manage this more sustainably?

   - _____
   - _____
   - _____

Notes & Personal Insights

Use this space to capture thoughts, patterns, or insights as you continue your Career Resilience & Wellness journey.

- _____
- _____
- _____
- _____
- _____
- _____

CHAPTER THREE

Regulation, Not Suppression

You cannot always control what happens around you, but you can control how you regulate what happens within you.

In many workplaces, people are taught, directly or indirectly, to suppress emotions. Phrases such as "stay professional," "push through," or "leave it at the door" are often used as guidance. While these messages may be well intentioned, emotional suppression is not emotional intelligence, and it is not a sustainable strategy for long-term career success.

Career resilience is not about ignoring emotions. It is about regulating them. Emotional regulation allows us to recognize what we are feeling, understand why we are feeling it, and intentionally choose how we respond, without allowing emotions to control our behavior, drain our energy, or damage relationships.

Suppression vs. Regulation

Suppression occurs when emotions are pushed aside, minimized, or ignored. People may continue functioning outwardly, but emotional load accumulates internally.

Over time, suppression can lead to:

- Emotional exhaustion
- Irritability or withdrawal
- Reduced focus and patience
- Burnout that appears sudden but has been building over time

Regulation, on the other hand, is an active skill. It acknowledges emotions without being ruled by them.

Regulation says:
- I notice what I am feeling.
- I understand what triggered it.
- I decide how to move forward.

This distinction is essential in today's workplace, where uncertainty, rapid change, and emotional demands are constant.

Why Regulation Is a Career Skill

Post-COVID work environments have elevated emotional regulation from a "soft skill" to a core professional competency. Hybrid schedules, evolving expectations, unreliable technology, staffing gaps, and unfinished workplace transitions all contribute to emotional strain.

Without regulation:
- Small frustrations escalate.
- Communication breaks down.
- Decisions become reactive.
- Relationships suffer.

With regulation:
- Professionals maintain composure under pressure.
- Leaders foster psychological safety.
- Teams recover more quickly from disruption.
- Individuals protect mental health while remaining productive.

In my work with youth and adults navigating disabilities, regulation is often the difference between persistence and shutdown. That same truth now applies across the modern workforce.

Self-regulation is the bridge between emotional awareness and effective action.

A Practical Regulation Model

Emotional regulation does not require perfection. It requires practice.

Step 1: Notice the Signal

Emotions often appear physically before we recognize them mentally.

Common signals include:
- Tight shoulders or jaw
- Shallow breathing
- Racing thoughts
- Sudden fatigue or irritability

The moment you notice the signal, regulation has already begun.

Step 2: Pause the Reaction

A brief pause creates space between emotion and action.

This pause may look like:
- Taking a deep breath
- Counting slowly
- Standing or changing posture
- Delaying a response

Pausing interrupts automatic reactions and restores choice.

Step 3: Name the Emotion

Naming emotions reduces their intensity and increases clarity.

Examples:

- "I am frustrated because expectations changed."
- "I am anxious because information is unclear."
- "I am overwhelmed because I am carrying multiple roles." This step transforms emotion into usable information.

Step 4: Choose the Response Once regulated, ask:
- What response aligns with my values?
- What response protects my energy?
- What response moves this situation forward?

This is where emotional intelligence becomes professional leadership.

Practical Illustration: Regulation in a Hybrid Work Breakdown

Marcus had recently returned to the office two days a week after working remotely for three years. On his first day back, meeting rooms were unavailable, technology failed repeatedly, and a client presentation was disrupted.

Marcus felt frustration building. His jaw tightened. His thoughts raced.

Instead of pushing through or reacting defensively, Marcus paused. He stepped away briefly, took several slow breaths, and acknowledged that his frustration was rooted in system limitations rather than personal failure.

Once regulated, he calmly communicated the issue, proposed a backup plan, and followed up with the client later that day.

The challenges remained, but Marcus preserved his professionalism and energy.

Career Resilience Lesson:

Regulation does not remove challenges. It prevents escalation.

Practical Illustration: Regulation and Self-Advocacy

Tanya, a capable professional with a cognitive processing disability, struggled during a fast-paced meeting where expectations shifted repeatedly without clarification.

She felt anxious and overwhelmed. In the past, she would have stayed silent and blamed herself later.

This time, Tanya noticed her physical signals, paused, grounded herself, and calmly asked for clarification. She followed up with written notes to confirm understanding. Rather than suppressing her response, Tanya regulated it and advocated for clarity without apology.

Regulation supports self-advocacy. Suppression erodes confidence.

Coach Ella Says

You are not required to absorb chaos to prove your capability. Regulation allows you to stay present without carrying what does not belong to you.

Reflection: Your Regulation Patterns

Take a moment to reflect.

1. What physical or emotional signals tell me I am becoming dysregulated?

-
-
-
-

2. In what situations do I tend to suppress emotions rather than regulate them?

- _____
- _____
- _____

3. What helps me pause before reacting, such as breathing, movement, silence, or time?

- _____
- _____

4. How might stronger regulation improve my communication, decision-making, or well-being?

- _____
- _____

Notes & Personal Insights

- _____
- _____
- _____
- _____

Closing Thought

The most resilient professionals are not the ones who feel the least. They are the ones who recover the fastest.

CHAPTER FOUR

Boundaries, Capacity, and Sustainable Performance

You do not build a lasting career by doing everything. You build it by knowing what to hold and what to release.

For many professionals, boundaries feel uncomfortable. They worry that setting limits will be seen as a lack of commitment, a poor attitude, or an unwillingness to be a team player. For others, especially those who have spent years navigating systems that required constant adjustment, boundaries may feel like a luxury rather than a necessity. In today's workplace, boundaries are no longer optional. They are a core part of career resilience and wellness. Boundaries protect your capacity, and capacity determines your sustainability.

Capacity Is Not Character

One of the most damaging myths in the workplace is the belief that capacity reflects character. When people feel overwhelmed, they often internalize stress as a personal shortcoming rather than recognizing situational strain.

Capacity is influenced by:

- Workload and role clarity
- Access to resources and support
- Health, caregiving, and life responsibilities
- Environmental and system readiness

None of these define your worth.

When capacity is exceeded for too long, even the most capable professionals begin to struggle, not because they are weak, but because they are human.

Boundaries as an Act of Self-Leadership

Boundaries are often misunderstood as walls. They are clear signals and guidelines that allow you to show up consistently without depletion.

Healthy boundaries:

- Clarify expectations
- Reduce resentment
- Improve communication
- Preserve energy and focus

They also model emotional intelligence and professionalism, especially for teams and emerging professionals who are learning how to manage themselves in complex environments.

Coach Ella Says

Boundaries are not about saying no to people. They are about saying yes to your long-term wellbeing.

Recognizing When Boundaries Are Needed

Boundaries become necessary when warning signs appear.

Common indicators include:

- Chronic fatigue or irritability
- Difficulty concentrating
- Feeling emotionally reactive or disconnected
- Growing resentment toward tasks or people
- Loss of joy or motivation These signals are not failures. They are information.

Listening early prevents burnout later.

Soft Boundaries That Still Work

Not all boundaries need to be firm lines. Some are soft boundaries, small adjustments that reduce strain without confrontation.

Examples include:

- Clarifying priorities before accepting new tasks
- Asking for timelines instead of assuming urgency
- Creating response windows instead of constant availability
- Structuring the day to protect focus and recover time

In settings that demand adaptability, or where direct limits are challenging due to power imbalances, soft boundaries prove particularly beneficial.

<u>Practical Illustration: Choosing Capacity Over Guilt</u>

Angela was known as the dependable one. Whenever gaps appeared, she filled them, staying late, adjusting schedules, and quietly absorbing additional responsibilities.

Over time, Angela noticed she was exhausted and increasingly resentful. The work she once enjoyed felt heavy.

Instead of abruptly refusing requests, Angela practiced soft boundaries. She began asking clarifying questions:

- "What is the priority level of this?"
- "What can shift if I take this on?"
- "What is the timeline?"

By slowing the pace of commitment, Angela protected her capacity without damaging trust.

Career Resilience Lesson:

Sustainability grows when boundaries are proactive, not reactive.

Boundaries Through a Different-Ability Lens

People bring different abilities, processing styles, health needs, and energy patterns into the workplace. Sustainable performance requires honoring those differences, not ignoring them.

Some professionals manage sensory overload, fluctuating energy, chronic conditions, or processing differences. Others balance caregiving responsibilities, mental health needs, or recovery from illness or injury. These realities shape how capacity is experienced.

Advocating for boundaries does not mean lowering expectations. It means aligning expectations with reality.

When workplaces normalize boundaries, they create environments where more people can perform well, contribute meaningfully, and remain engaged over time.

Practical Illustration: Boundary-Setting as Self-Advocacy

Jamal was a skilled professional who managed his work alongside ongoing health considerations. Back-to-back virtual meetings left him mentally and physically depleted, affecting his focus later in the day.

Rather than pushing through, Jamal requested short breaks between meetings and followed up key discussions in writing. He framed his request around performance, clarity, and sustainability.

The result was improved concentration, stronger communication, and consistent results, without burnout.

Career Resilience Lesson:

Boundaries enable performance. They do not limit it.

Coach Ella Says

You do not owe anyone burnout. You owe yourself sustainability. Reflection: Your Boundaries and Capacity Pause and reflect.

1. Where am I currently operating beyond my capacity?

   _____

   _____

2. What signals tell me it is time to pause or adjust?

   _____

   _____

3. What is one soft boundary I could introduce right now?

   _____

   _____

How would honoring my capacity improve my work and well-being?

   _____

   _____

   _____

Notes & Personal Insights

   _____

   _____

   _____

   _____

.Closing Thought

Sustainable success is not about how much you give. It is about how wisely you protect what allows you to keep giving.

CHAPTER FIVE

Recovery, Rest, and Rebuilding Energy

Rest is not quitting. It is how you make room to continue.

In many work cultures, rest is misunderstood. It is often treated as a reward for exhaustion, something to be earned after productivity has been proven. This mindset leads people to push past healthy limits, believing that slowing down signals' weakness or lack of commitment.

Career resilience offers a different truth. Rest is not the opposite of performance. It is what sustains performance.

Recovery allows your mind and body to reset, recalibrate, and regain the energy required to think clearly, communicate effectively, and respond thoughtfully in demanding environments.

Why Recovery Matters More Than Ever

Today's work rarely has a clear stopping point. Technology keeps us reachable, expectations shift quickly, and many people carry emotional and cognitive loads long after the workday ends.

Without intentional recovery:

- Focus declines.
- Patience wears thin.
- Emotional regulation becomes harder.
- Motivation fades.

Recovery restores what constant effort depletes. This is especially important for individuals managing different abilities, health needs, or fluctuating energy levels, but it applies to everyone navigating modern work.

Rest Is Not One Size Fits All

Rest does not always mean sleep or time off. True recovery comes in many forms, and each person must learn what genuinely restores them.

Examples include:

- Mental rest: stepping away from problem solving and decision making.
- Emotional rest: limiting draining conversations or environments.
- Physical rest: honoring fatigue, tension, or pain signals.
- Sensory rest: reducing noise, screen time, or stimulation.
- Social rest: choosing solitude or low demand connection.

Effective recovery aligns with your needs, not someone else's expectations.

Coach Ella Says

You don't need permission to rest. Your capacity already told you.

Micro Recovery: Small Resets That Add Up

Recovery does not always require long breaks. Small, intentional resets throughout the day can significantly reduce fatigue.

Micro recovery practices may include:

- Standing and stretching between tasks. • Taking a few deep breaths before responding.
- Stepping outside or changing environments.
- Pausing screens for a few minutes.
- Drinking water and grounding physically.

These moments may seem minor, but over time they protect your energy and clarity.

Practical Illustration: Rebuilding Energy Without Stepping Away

Carlos was committed to his role but noticed his energy dropping by midafternoon. He felt foggy, impatient, and less engaged during meetings. Instead of pushing harder, Carlos experimented with micro recovery. He blocked ten minutes between meetings, stepped outside when possible, and stopped multitasking during lunch.

Within weeks, his focus improved and his work felt manageable again.

Career Resilience Lesson:

Recovery doesn't require retreat. It requires intention.

Recovery and Different Abilities

People experience energy differently. Some require predictable routines. Others need flexibility, quiet spaces, or recovery time after high focus work. Recognizing these differences allows professionals to design workdays that support sustainability.

Honoring recovery is not an accommodation. It is a strategy for consistency and excellence.

When individuals are supported in managing energy, teams benefit from clearer thinking, better collaboration, and fewer breakdowns.

Practical Illustration: Rest as a Leadership Skill

Monica, a team leader, noticed rising tension and disengagement across her staff. Rather than increasing pressure, she normalized recovery. Meetings became shorter, focus time was protected, and realistic timelines were reinforced.

The result was not less productivity, but better outcomes, fewer errors, and stronger morale.

Career Resilience Lesson:

Leaders who value recovery create resilient teams.

Coach Ella Says

Burnout doesn't come from caring too much. It comes from resting too little.

Reflection: Your Recovery Patterns

Take a moment to pause.

1. How do I know when my energy is depleted?

_____

_____

2. What currently drains me the most during my workday?

_____

_____

3. What helps me recover, physically, mentally, or emotionally?

_____

_____

4. What is one small recovery practice I could begin this week?

_____

_____

Notes & Personal Insights

_____

_____

_____

_____

_____

Closing Thought

You don't rebuild energy by pushing through depletion. You rebuild it by honoring the signals that tell you to pause..

CHAPTER SIX

Communication That Preserves Trust Under Pressure

Pressure doesn't reveal who we are. It reveals how supported we feel.

When pressure increases, communication is often the first thing to suffer. Even strong relationships can feel strained when expectations shift, emotions run high, or energy is depleted. Words may come out sharper than intended. Silence may replace engagement. Trust can weaken, not because people don't care, but because stress is speaking louder than intention.

Career resilience is not about communicating perfectly. It is about communicating in ways that preserve trust, connection, and emotional safety, even when conditions are challenging.

Why Pressure Changes the Way We Relate

Under pressure, the nervous system shifts into efficient mode. The brain prioritizes speed over empathy, reaction over reflection. This can show up as:

- Shortened patience
- Misinterpreted tone
- Defensive responses
- Withholding rather than sharing

In today's workplace, where conversations often happen through email, text, or video, connection can break down quickly. Without awareness, pressure-driven communication can unintentionally damage relationships that matter.

Recognizing this dynamic allows us to slow the moment and respond with intention.

Regulation Comes Before Connection

Healthy communication under pressure begins internally.

When emotions rise, connection weakens unless we pause first.

Before responding:

- Breathe
- Ground yourself
- Acknowledge what you are feeling

Regulation restores choice, and choice protects relationships.

Coach Ella Says

If you want to protect the relationship, regulate yourself first.

Communicating to Maintain Trust is preserved when people feel:

- Heard
- Respected
- Valued
- Safe to clarify

Under pressure, trust grows when communication is:

- Clear rather than charged
- Curious rather than assumptive
- Direct but compassionate

This does not require perfect wording, just presence. For example, instead of reacting with frustration:

- "This doesn't make sense"

Try grounding the conversation:

- "I need a little more clarity so I can respond well"

Small shifts like this reduce defensiveness and keep connection intact.

Listening as a Wellness Practice

Listening under pressure is not about fixing. It is about staying connected.

When people feel stressed, being truly heard can lower emotional intensity and restore balance. Listening allows space for understanding before action.

Healthy listening includes:

- Giving full attention
- Allowing pauses
- Reflecting what you hear
- Asking open, supportive questions Listening does not mean agreement.

It means respect and emotional presence.

Practical Illustration: Choosing Connection Over Reaction

Denise received a brief, urgent email late in the day requesting immediate changes to a project. She felt overlooked and pressured.

Instead of responding immediately, Denise paused. She regulated her emotions overnight and replied the next morning with a calm message asking for clarity around priorities and timelines.

The response shifted the tone of the conversation and preserved trust.

Career Resilience Lesson:

Connection grows when response replaces reaction.

Honoring Different Communication Needs

People process information differently, especially under stress. Some need time to reflect. Others need written follow-up. Some communicate best verbally; others prefer structure and predictability.

Resilient communication adapts without judgment.

When professionals acknowledge different communication needs, they strengthen inclusion, reduce misalignment, and protect emotional well-being for everyone involved.

Practical Illustration: Inquiry That Builds Understanding

Evan noticed a colleague becoming unusually quiet during meetings. Rather than assuming disengagement, he checked in privately.

The colleague shared that they were overwhelmed by rapid changes and benefited from written summaries.

That small adjustment restored participation and trust.

Career Resilience Lesson:

Inquiry creates understanding, and understanding supports wellness.

Coach Ella Says

Effective communication doesn't rush understanding. It makes room for it.

.

.

.

.

Reflection: Communication and Connection

Pause and reflect.

- How do I typically communicate when I feel pressured or emotionally loaded?

  .
  _____
  .
  _____
  .
  _____

- What helps me pause before responding in challenging moments?

  .
  _____
  .
  _____
  .
  _____

- How can I communicate in ways that protect trust, even when I am stressed?

  .
  _____
  .
  _____
  .
  _____

- What listening habits could strengthen my relationships at work?

  .
  _____
  .
  _____
  .
  .

Notes & Personal Insights

-
-
-
-
-
-
-

Closing Thought

When communication protects trust, resilience follows.

CHAPTER SEVEN

Navigating Change Without Losing Yourself

Change doesn't require permission. What matters is how you meet it.

Change has become a constant companion in today's workplace. Roles evolve. Expectations shift. Technology updates midstream. Workspaces change before people are ready. For many professionals, the pace of change feels relentless, leaving little time to process what is happening, let alone adapt with confidence.

Career resilience is not about resisting change. It is about navigating it without losing clarity, confidence, or self-trust.

Why Change Feels So Heavy

Change creates emotional and cognitive load because it disrupts what once felt predictable. Even positive change can trigger uncertainty, fatigue, and self-doubt.

Common reactions include:

- Feeling unsteady or behind
- Questioning your competence
- Frustration with unclear direction
- Anxiety about keeping up

These reactions are human, not signs that something is wrong with you.

What matters most is not how quickly you adapt, but how intentionally you respond.

Start with Situation Awareness

Before reacting to change, pause and assess what is happening. Situation analysis allows you to separate facts from fear and regain a sense of control.

Ask yourself:

- What has changed, specifically?
- What remains within my control?
- What is unclear versus unknown?
- What assumptions might I be making?

Clarity reduces emotional overwhelm and creates a foundation for wise decisions.

Coach Ella Says

You can't respond well to change until you understand what you are responding to.

Learning New Skills Without Self-Judgment

Change often requires new technical, emotional, or relational skills. Learning something new can stir discomfort, especially for seasoned professionals who are used to feeling competent.

Growth does not mean starting over. It means building forward.

Approach skill development with curiosity instead of criticism:

- Identify what the moment is asking you to learn
- Focus on progress, not perfection
- Allow yourself to be a learner again

Learning under pressure is challenging, but it is also a powerful resilience muscle.

Practical Illustration: Reframing Skill Gaps

Diane had been in her role for over a decade when new software was introduced. She felt embarrassed asking questions and worried others were adapting faster.

Instead of withdrawing, Diane reframed the situation. She identified specific gaps, scheduled short learning sessions, and practiced without pressure to master everything at once.

Over time, confidence returned, and so did her sense of capability.

Career Resilience Lesson:

Learning is not a setback. It is a strategy.

Dealing with Challenges as Ongoing Conditions

Some challenges are temporary. Others persist.

Career resilience means learning how to function well even when conditions are not ideal. This includes navigating:

- Ongoing uncertainty
- Resource limitations
- Incomplete systems
- Repeated adjustments

Rather than waiting for things to settle, resilient professionals build rhythms that allow them to stay grounded amid instability.

This may include:

- Regular check-ins with yourself
- Clear personal priorities
- Supportive routines

- Honest communication

Stability does not always come from the environment. It often comes from within.

Practical Illustration: Staying Grounded Through Ongoing Change

Malik worked in an organization undergoing repeated restructuring. Just as teams adjusted, another change followed.

Instead of burning out, Malik focused on what anchored him: clear values, manageable routines, and realistic expectations. He stayed informed without obsessing and focused on what he could influence.

This approach helped him remain steady and effective while others grew discouraged.

Career Resilience Lesson:

Grounding yourself creates stability, even when the system does not.

Coach Ella Says

You don't need all the answers to move forward. You need awareness, willingness, and self-trust.

Reflection: Your Relationship with Change

Take a moment to reflect.

- What changes am I currently navigating?

.
_____
.
_____
.

.

- What emotions does this change bring for me?

- What skills or adjustments might this season be asking me to develop?

- What helps me stay grounded when things feel uncertain?

Notes & Personal Insights

Closing Thought

Resilience is not about avoiding change. It is about moving through it with clarity and care..

CHAPTER EIGHT

Confidence, Self-Trust, and Moving Forward

Confidence doesn't come from certainty. It comes from trusting yourself through uncertainty.

Confidence is often misunderstood as boldness, certainty, or having all the answers. True confidence is quieter and far more resilient. It shows up as self-trust: the belief that you can respond, adjust, and recover no matter what comes next.

In today's changing workplace, confidence is less about control and more about grounding.

Career resilience grows when confidence is rooted in self-awareness, experience, and choice, rather than perfection or external validation.

When Confidence Gets Shaken

Change, disruption, and prolonged stress can quietly erode confidence. People may begin to question themselves not because they lack skill, but because the environment keeps shifting.

Confidence often weakens when:

- Expectations change without clarity
- Feedback feels inconsistent or impersonal
- Systems are incomplete or unreliable
- Energy is depleted over time

These experiences can cause capable professionals to doubt themselves unnecessarily. Recognizing this dynamic is the first step in restoring confidence.

Self-Trust as the Foundation

Self-trust is the belief that you can:

- Make reasonable decisions
- Learn what you don't yet know
- Adjust when something doesn't work
- Advocate for what you need

Self-trust grows through experience, not by avoiding mistakes. Each time you navigate a challenge, pause, reflect, and respond intentionally, you reinforce your own reliability.

Coach Ella Says

You don't lose confidence because you're incapable. You lose it when you stop trusting yourself.

Confidence Through Reflection, Not Comparison

One of the fastest ways to weaken confidence is comparison, especially in environments where productivity, adaptability, or visibility are constantly measured.

Resilient confidence comes from reflection instead of comparison.

Ask yourself:

- What have I handled before?
- What skills have I already built?
- What challenges have I survived and learned from?

Confidence strengthens when you recognize your own progress even when it is not perfect or public.

Practical Illustration: Reclaiming Confidence After Change

Nicole had recently transitioned into a role that looked familiar on paper but felt quite different in practice. New tools, new expectations, and a different leadership style left her second-guessing herself.

Instead of pushing harder, Nicole paused. She reflected on her past successes, identified what skills still applied, and gave herself permission to learn what was new.

Over time, confidence returned not because the job became easier, but because she trusted herself again.

Career Resilience Lesson:

Confidence grows when self-trust leads the way.

Moving Forward Without Overthinking

Forward movement does not require certainty. It requires intention.

Rather than asking:

- "Am I ready?"

Try asking:

- "What's the next reasonable step?"

Small, thoughtful steps rebuild momentum and reinforce confidence without overwhelm.

Moving forward might mean:

- Trying something new imperfectly
- Asking for support
- Clarifying expectations
- Adjusting your pace

Progress is often quieter than we expect, but no less meaningful.

Practical Illustration: Choosing Progress Over Perfection

Andre felt stuck after multiple changes at work. He kept waiting for clarity before acting.

Eventually, Andre shifted his approach. He chose one manageable action each week, updating a skill, having a conversation, or refining a process.

Those small steps restored momentum and confidence.

Career Resilience Lesson:

Progress builds confidence. Perfection delays it.

Coach Ella Says

You don't have to feel confident moving forward. You must just trust yourself enough to begin.

Reflection: Strengthening Self-Trust

Take a moment to reflect.

- When do I feel most confident, and why?

  _____

  _____

- What experiences remind me that I am capable?

  _____

  _____

- Where might I be waiting for certainty instead of trusting myself?

  _____

  _____

- .What is one small step I can take to move forward this week?

Notes & Personal Insights

Closing Thought

Confidence is not about having control. It is about trusting yourself to respond when control is not possible.

CHAPTER NINE

Purpose, Meaning, and Staying Engaged

Purpose doesn't disappear during hard seasons. It gets quieter. Engagement is how we listen to it.

When work becomes demanding, unpredictable, or emotionally heavy, people often begin to disengage, not because they no longer care, but because they are protecting themselves. Engagement fades when energy is low, trust feels shaky, or meaning feels disconnected from daily tasks.

Career resilience is not just about endurance. It is about staying connected to purpose without burning out.

Purpose does not require loving every task. It requires remembering why your work still matters to you.

When Engagement Starts to Slip

Disengagement rarely happens overnight. It tends to show up gradually.

You may notice:

- Going through the motions
- Reduced curiosity or creativity
- Emotional distance from work or colleagues
- A sense of "just getting through the day" These signals are not failures.

They are invitations to pause and reconnect.

Purpose Is Personal and It Evolves

Purpose is not a fixed destination. It changes as life changes.

At various stages, purpose may look like:

- Stability
- Growth
- Service
- Learning
- Balance
- Contribution without overextension

Comparing your purpose to someone else's path often leads to frustration. Resilient engagement comes from honoring where you are now, not where you think you should be.

Coach Ella Says

Purpose isn't about doing more. It's about caring with intention.

Finding Meaning in Everyday Work

Not every role feels inspiring every day. Meaning often lives in small, overlooked moments:

- Helping someone move forward
- Creating clarity where there was confusion
- Showing up with integrity
- Supporting others through change

Meaning grows when you notice impact, not just outcomes.

Ask yourself:

- Who benefits from my work?
- Where do I make things easier, clearer, or better?
- What values do I bring into my role?

These reflections reconnect effort to purpose.

Practical Illustration: Re-engaging Without Overcommitting

Samantha loved her work. After multiple changes, she felt disconnected. Instead of taking on more responsibility to "feel useful," she paused.

She identified one part of her role that aligned with her values and focused her energy there. She reconnected with colleagues she enjoyed collaborating with and let go of unnecessary pressure.

Engagement returned, not because the workload changed, but because meaning did.

Career Resilience Lesson:

Engagement grows when purpose is protected.

Staying Engaged During Uncertain Seasons

Sometimes, purpose feels distant because the future feels unclear. During these seasons, staying engaged doesn't mean forcing motivation. It means maintaining connection.

Ways to stay engaged without draining yourself:

- Focus on what you can influence today
- Keep learning, even informally
- Maintain relationships that energize you
- Acknowledge progress, not just completion Engagement does not require certainty.

It requires presence.

Practical Illustration: Purpose Through Presence

Derrick worked in a department facing ongoing uncertainty. Long-term plans kept changing, and morale was low.

Instead of disengaging, Derrick focused on being present with his team, offering support, listening, and maintaining steady communication. His consistency became a source of stability for others.

Career Resilience Lesson:

Purpose often shows up through how you treat people, especially during uncertainty.

Coach Ella Says

You don't lose purpose because things get hard. You lose it when you stop noticing your impact.

<u>Reflection: Reconnecting with Meaning</u>

Take a moment to reflect.

- When do I feel most engaged in my work and why?

_____

_____

- What values do I bring into my role, regardless of the title?

_____

_____

- Where might I be disengaging to protect myself?

_____

_____

- What small action could help me reconnect with meaning this week?

Notes & Personal Insights

Closing Thought

Engagement isn't about constant passion. It's about staying connected to what matters, even quietly.

CHAPTER TEN

Sustaining Yourself Over Time

Resilience is not something you turn on during a crisis and turn off once things improve. It is something you practice quietly over time, often without realizing it, through the choices you make about pace, boundaries, and self-care.

Earlier chapters focused on understanding change, managing disruption, and rebuilding confidence. This chapter moves beyond response and into sustainability, how you continue forward without burning out, hardening, or losing yourself in the process.

Career resilience is not about pushing through endlessly. It is about learning how to last well.

The Difference Between Endurance and Sustainability

Many people confuse resilience with endurance. Endurance is about surviving. Sustainability is about continuing.

You can endure difficult seasons through effort and determination alone, but sustainability requires something more thoughtful. It requires you to pay attention to your energy, your values, and the rhythms of your life, not just your goals.

Over time, resilience becomes less about reacting to change and more about designing a life and career that can absorb change without constant strain.

Practical Illustration: Carrying the Load

Imagine carrying a heavy bag over a long distance. At first, you adjust your grip and keep moving. But if you never stop to redistribute the weight, rest your shoulders, or set the bag down briefly, the strain builds.

Careers work the same way.

Resilient people learn when to carry the load, when to shift it, and when to rest without guilt.

Building Habits That Support Longevity

Sustaining yourself over time is less about big interventions and more about consistent, manageable practices.

This might look like:

- Setting realistic expectations for yourself
- Creating routines that support focus and recovery
- Recognizing early signs of fatigue or frustration
- Choosing boundaries that protect your energy
- Staying connected to people and practices that ground you

These habits are not signing of weakness. They are signs of wisdom.

Coach Ella Says

Resilience isn't about doing more. It's about knowing what you need to continue.

Staying Connected to Purpose and Values

Long-term resilience depends on meaning.

When work becomes disconnected from purpose or values, even small challenges can feel overwhelming. When your work aligns with what matters to you, you are better able to navigate change without losing motivation or identity.

This does not require having everything figured out. It requires returning again and again to questions like:

- What matters most to me right now?

- What kind of life am I trying to build?
- What am I willing to protect, even during busy seasons?

Purpose provides direction. Values provide stability.

Reflection: Sustaining Your Path

Take a moment to reflect:

- What currently helps you feel steady and supported?
- Where do you notice strain building over time?
- What habits or boundaries would help you continue more sustainably?
- How do your current choices align with your values?

Resilience grows when reflection becomes a regular practice, not an emergency response.

Moving Forward with Care

As you move forward, remember that resilience is not a destination you reach once and for all. It is a way of moving through life and work with awareness, compassion, and intention.

You are allowed to adjust your pace. You are allowed to redefine success.

You are allowed to care for yourself while still growing.

Sustaining yourself over time is not about avoiding difficulty. It is about learning how to meet it without losing your sense of self.

Resilience is not loud. It is steady.

And it is built one thoughtful choice at a time.

.

Editor's Confirmation (for your confidence)

You have reached the end of this book, but not the end of your journey.

Career resilience and wellness are not destinations you arrive at once. They are practice shaped by seasons, strengthened by experience, and refined through reflection. The tools you've explored here are not meant to be used all at once or perfectly. They are meant to meet you where you are.

If this book has done its work, you may feel more grounded. More aware. More compassionate with yourself. That matters.

The workplace will continue to change. Systems may remain imperfect. Expectations will shift. What does not have to shift is your ability to respond with intention rather than urgency, with clarity rather than fear, and with care rather than depletion.

Your career does not need to cost you your wellbeing.

As you move forward, I invite you to do three things simply and consistently.

First, choose awareness.

Pay attention to your capacity, your energy, and your emotional load. Awareness is the beginning of wise action.

Second, choose alignment.

Let your values, boundaries, and purpose guide your decisions. Alignment creates sustainability.

Third, choose yourself without guilt.

Rest when needed. Ask questions. Learn at your pace. Advocate for what supports your success.

Career resilience is not about pushing harder.

It is about moving forward with care, courage, and clarity. You are allowed to grow without losing yourself.

Coach Ella Says

- Success that makes you healthy is too expensive.
- Carry what serves you.
- Release what no longer fits.

And move forward knowing you are capable, adaptable, and worthy of a career that supports your whole life.

With confidence in your journey, Coach Ella

Final Reflection Workbook

Your Career Resilience & Wellness Plan

This concluding section is your space to pause, reflect, and intentionally shape what comes next. There are no right or wrong answers, only honest ones.

Return to these pages whenever you need grounding, clarity, or recalibration.

Part One: Looking Back with Compassion

- What insights from this book resonated most with me? Why?

_____
_____

- What patterns or habits did I recognize in myself?

_____
_____

- What strengths have I relied on more than I realized?

_____
_____
_____

Part Two: Understanding My Current Season

- How would I describe my current career season?
- ☐ Growth
- ☐ Transition
- ☐ Stabilization
- ☐ Recovery
- ☐ Exploration
- ☐ Other:
- What is currently supporting my wellbeing?

_____
_____

- What is currently draining my energy or focus?

_____
_____
_____

Part Three: Resilience & Wellness Check-In

- How am I doing in these areas?

Area	Needs Attention	Stable	Strong
Boundaries	☐	☐	☐
Energy & Recovery	☐	☐	☐
Communication	☐	☐	☐
Confidence & Self-Trust	☐	☐	☐
Purpose & Engagement	☐	☐	☐

- What is one small adjustment that would improve my overall wellbeing?

_____

_____

_____

Part Four: Learning, Growth, and Agility

- What skill, mindset, or habit would support my next season?

- How do I prefer to learn when under pressure?

- What does career agility look like for me right now?

Part Five: Moving Forward with Intention

- What boundaries do I need to protect moving forward?

- How will I know when it's time to pause or adjust?

- What does sustainable success look like for me now?

My Commitment to Myself

In this next season, I commit to:

- _____
- _____

Signature (optional): _____   Date: _____

- _____
- _____
-

Final Coach Ella Reminder

You have the right to create a career that enhances your life rather than challenges it.

ABOUT THE AUTHOR

Ella L. Clark is an entrepreneur, certified career coach, and leadership development professional with more than four decades of experience helping individuals and organizations navigate career growth, transition, and change.

She is the Founder and CEO of The Clark Group, LLC, where she partners with schools, nonprofits, and employers to strengthen workforce readiness, leadership capacity, and career sustainability.

Through her writing, coaching, and training, Ella helps people move forward with clarity, confidence, and purpose.

www.ingramcontent.com/pod-product-compliance
Lightning Source LLC
LaVergne TN
LVHW020939090426
835512LV00020B/3430